FRANCHISING MADE EASY

I0511275

"The 3 Things You Need to Learn Before You Begin Franchising in Mexico"

ISBN: 978-1512285062
ISBN: 1512285064

TABLE OF CONTENTS

TESTIMONIALS

"I can finally say with confidence I have found a company providing the importation services needed to successfully ensure proper border-crossing of goods with every shipment into Mexico. With facilities on both sides of the border, Nery's Logistics has perfected the art of consolidating product in the U.S., clearing customs, and efficiently distributing throughout Mexico all while providing excellent service and clear communication throughout. As a chain that has now tested 5 different supply chains on both land and sea, Nery's has answered our call for help by providing a 'one-stop solution' for all the franchisee's distribution needs."

Thomas Davis - Global Sourcing & Supply Chain Administrator. Front Burner Brands - The Melting Pot

"Sandro Piancone, and his company have built a best in class supply chain organization to support the Little Caesar Pizza chain throughout the country of Mexico. They invested in people, warehouse's, and transportation related asset's to provide complete service for both food and restaurant equipment to allow the LCE franchise system in Mexico to grow and flourish. Furthermore through strategic processes they executed a national pricing plan to ensure every franchise owner paid the same price of goods to allow each store to realize solid profitability. I can't say enough of Sandro Piancone and his staff, on their confidence and resources they command to work as a partner in supply chain responsibilities."

Matt Ilitch - Former President of Blue Line Foodservice Distribution

"In the world of pretend experts, Sandro is a breath of fresh air. He is a master of showing you, in a step-by-step, no-nonsense, no fluff manner how to franchise in Mexico. His passion and knowledge for this exudes from every page. If you ever thought about doing business in Mexico, this is your playbook."

Dave Dee - Chief Marketing Officer, GKIC.com

"As the Senior Director of Purchasing and R & D for Villa Enterprises, a 350 restaurant chain for the past 9 years, exporting and distribution in Mexico has been my most challenging responsibility. Unbelievably, it is easier to send containers to Kuwait than it is to export to Mexico. And there's no water separating US and Mexico! After many months struggling with this challenge, I was finally introduced to Sandro Piancone about a year ago. In those 12 short months, Sandro has given my company the option of full broad line distribution in Mexico with all of our printed and proprietary items, with full visibility. Included with that service is extensive communication to our operations team in Mexico and the US. Sandro outshines his competitors with reporting capabilities that are not offered by any other exporting or distribution option. It has become a truly mutually beneficial partnership with honest, open communication. A relationship in which each side has a vested interest in the other."

Michael Rosen, Sr. Director of Purchasing and R & D, Villa Enterprises Management

"As someone who lives in the US, we often forget what a big world extends beyond our borders. Our biggest neighbor, Mexico, is a huge country affording a great opportunity for successful business owners and franchises to expand. This book is a great primer to do exactly that."

Henry Evans - Best-selling author, *The Hour A Day Entrepreneur* Founder, Timezone Marketing, Inc.

"My family has been in the food business since 1963 serving several large pizza chains and food service customers across the US. In 1993 I was a part of a FAS food expo in Mexico City sponsored by the Clinton administration. At that event I did everything wrong and spent 4 days at this expo with no samples, no Spanish and no plan. It wasn't until I met Mr. Piancone in 2012 that I realize what an opportunity there was selling in Mexico. So in 2014 I was invited to join the CEO tour in Guadalajara and attend the ANTAD convention and found that

that event was worth every penny and time I spent expanding our business in Mexico."

Patrick E. Spaulding – President Spaulding and Associates

"Sandro Piancone knowledge of how to be successful in Mexico is 'turnkey'. No one has done more 'due diligence' than he – he has figured out the biggest 'disastrous first steps' down to the smallest 'how did he know that?' detail. Any company who chooses to enter Mexico without following his 'Mexpert' guidance will not only never achieve peak performance – they may not be in existence down the road. A MUST read!"

Don Vlcek - Marco's Franchising LLC, Vice President of Purchasing. President, Marco's Pizza Distribution LLC

Introduction

Meet the MEXPERT

Hi my name is Sandro Piancone. I am the Chief Mexpert officer of Mexico Franchising Made Easy. And if you are wondering, yes, Mexpert is a real word: or at least it is now. I trademarked it. I am called the Mexpert for a reason. Not because I have a degree in selling in Mexico, or have a degree in International business or finance, but because I have made more mistakes than anyone reading this book, and I've spent more money making those mistakes so that you don't have to. I could write a Novel just on the mistakes I have made. I and my team will make sure you and your company does not make the same mistakes that I have made over the last 14 years.

Of course while making those mistakes, I also had some home runs and grand slams. Since 1998, I have generated well over 500 million dollars in sales and profits for my clients and partners helping them export their products into Mexico and open up franchise businesses in Mexico. *That is why I titled this book, The 3 Things you need to learn before you begin franchising in Mexico.* My clients have found their riches in Mexico, why not you? Read on.....

In my bio, it says that I am a recovering CEO of a publicly traded food distribution company in Mexico. I took an idea and turned it into the first nationwide distributor of imported products into Mexico, going from 0 to $100 million dollars a year in just under 3 years. But that is a story for another day and another book: the wounds are still too fresh.

I can't remember being as bullish about the opportunities for American companies looking to export and benefit from the franchise model to Mexico as I am today. It's not just the dynamics of the Mexican economy itself, but with the economy once more slowing in United States the opportunities on the international stage are ripe to be seized.

I always had my doubts about the downside of the free trade zone. Politicians that have tried to blame any weaknesses in our own economy on the mechanism of the NAFTA agreement have come and gone, but NAFTA is still here and, in fact, working tremendously well and doing what Presidents Reagan and Clinton believed it would.

One of Obama's central policies in the 2008 election campaign was taking apart NAFTA: a policy that, thankfully, has quietly disappeared.

But let's look at Mexico, and why I believe it is such a great place to do business now.

Over the last 20 years, Mexico has really started to pull its weight in the world. It's now the 11th largest global economy, and is pushing toward a top ten spot. The economy is now heavily weighted toward the services sector, and with such emphasis being placed on its education system the move toward a society reliant upon banking, finance, insurance, and retail is a given.

This in itself gives a great in for American exporters, not just of food and beverages, but also all manner of other goods aimed at a rapidly growing middle class consumer based. It's a young society, too, and one that is growing at over 1% each year. That's hardly a population explosion, but with the educational aspirations now inherent within the country, as well as the economic growth being seen now and through the future, the number of middle class consumers is likely to grow quite rapidly from the present 50 million or more. And that's a huge potential target market for all US businesses.

This potential is no more evident than in the franchise market, currently the fastest growing sector of the Mexican economy. In goods, foods, and services, franchise business growth is outstripping all others in Mexico, creating a new breed of Mexican entrepreneur.

Indeed, as an indication of the potential growth available, you just have to look at the growth of the Mexican economy and its retail sales. Mexico suffered a pretty horrendous collapse of its economy as a result of the global financial crisis. But it's a testament to the political stability of the nation, and good economic management, that she has recovered so rapidly and continues to grow much faster than its NAFTA neighbors. You know, the IMF forecasts for growth looking out two or three years puts Mexico up there with some of the fastest growth economies today. And that growth is available right on our doorstep, not across oceans and half way around the world.

I am also a fan of the way that the Mexican government has a real hand of control over its finances. Its budget deficit and net national debt is way below that of the United States, not just in absolute terms but more importantly in terms of respective GDP. This gives the Mexican government a huge fist to wield against any future economic shocks.

Times are tough in the United States, and look like being so for plenty of time to come. Taxes are rising, and government spending falling as the huge debt is tackled. Mexico doesn't face such problems. And that's good news for employment there, which is now below 5%, which in turn is good news for retail sales. And that's going to encourage plenty of imports from the United States. Then there is the huge opportunity we are now seeing caused by the opening up of Mexico's oil industry; itself considered to be a major contributor of growth for years to come.

So, all things considered, it's a great time to be doing business in Mexico. And that brings me to talking about how you can get involved if you're not already, and if you are, how you can improve procedures and processes that will get your product across the border and to the point of sale faster and more efficiently, allowing your franchise to roar to success.

I've been in business since I was a kid. I've built businesses from nothing and then sold them on as I moved to new challenges. A great part of my career history is grounded in the food and beverage business, and I've founded and grown fast food and traditional restaurant chains, as well as exporting companies. I suppose really that I was always looking for the business that presented me with the greatest satisfaction. And that's what I've found with Mexico Franchising Made Easy.

So it dawned on me that there are a whole lot of businesses not only making these mistakes, but also because of them they were being held back from making real riches in Mexico. And eventually, when they did find their products in place and ready to sell, margins had been shot to shreds because of the cost of those mistakes. To me, this was a great waste. So I decided to do something about it, and founded Mexico Franchising Made Easy.

One of the major mistakes that companies wanting to franchise in Mexico make is to jump in head first, without properly planning their entry into this lucrative market. You would not believe the amount of companies I meet at tradeshows that have spent 10s of thousands of dollars to exhibit at the show, but have not thought about trademarking their products, have done the NOM 51 labeling or even know the HS number of their products. They rush to set everything up, get orders on board, and then find that those orders can't be filled because they haven't first taken the time to complete the basic requirements of exporting to Mexico. Orders are lost and the business name is trashed before it even started.

That's what this book tackles, and the first thing that MSME tackles. We'll talk to you about your business, your goals, and your potential market. Then we'll do the required work of preparation for success. We'll take care of all your paperwork, ensuring your products are correctly classified, registering trademarks to protect your business from copycats, and making sure all your labeling conforms to current regulations.

Too many companies underestimate how difficult this process can be and how long it can take. Because we have so many years of experience behind us, and it's what we do every day of the week, every week of the year, we'll make this first part of the process as painless as possible.

Once these foundations for export have been put in place, then you can begin the real process of franchising in Mexico. And this is what you are good at: it's your product and your market. We consider it our duty to help you with this part of your business: after all, you are our client, and your success is our success. We can't become directly involved, but what we can do is give you the resources that you need to kick start your sales.

My second book, "Will My Product Sell In Mexico" concentrates many of its pages on this second stage of selling franchises in Mexico, which is selling, finding potential franchises, how to do tradeshows, giving tips on method of approach, who to approach, etc.

Finally, once you have your franchise model in place, now it's time for the business product sales. And here, we come back into the game, proactively working on your behalf.

We take care of all your import paperwork. After two decades of working with Mexican customs officials, we not only know and understand the rules, regulations, and methods, but we also know many of those officials as if they were our family. We work hand in hand with them to ensure your exports to Mexico flow smoothly.

We recommend a world class logistics company, Nery's Logistics, one of our Titanium clients" whose warehouses are among the best in the country. They'll ensure your goods move to their final destination as soon as possible, but while they await inspection and paperwork referencing they'll be guarded by 24 hour video surveillance, dedicated security guards, and the most comprehensive insurance package available.

Straight Talking in a Language You Understand

Many companies falsely believe that the Mexican market is closed to them because they don't speak Spanish.

Our representatives are experts in the importation of goods and services into Mexico. And they are tri-lingual: Spanish and English come natural to them, as does the language of importation law and customs jargon. We explain everything you need to know and more in plain English. That means you understand what is required, when and why. There's no ambiguity, no talking at cross purposes, and no accidents in translation.

Mexico Franchising Made Easy also ensures that you are kept up to date with any changes in laws or regulations. In fact, with our finger so firmly on the pulse of franchise and importation law and customs regulations, we often have advance knowledge of such changes. This means we can be proactive in our approach to your requirements for your exports and sales into Mexico.

Finally...

I'm so confident in Mexico as a place to sell to, and of MSFE's ability to help you with increasing your business, and profits, that I've put everything you need to know to begin exporting in this book.

And that, perhaps, is the whole point. That's how MSFE works. We work with you, our customer, keeping you fully informed of every step we take, and why we're taking it. Your business is selling. Our business is getting you and your product to the place where you can sell: Mexico.

Please feel free to visit MSFE's website, www.mexicofranchisingmadeeeasy.com, and find out more about the business, and how we can help you with your franchising in Mexico, and ask any questions you may have,

Regards

Sandro Piancone

Chief Mexpert Officer

Chapter 1

MEXICO – THE ECONOMY OF OPPORTUNITY FOR THE FRANCHISOR

Some facts you should know

Not too many people realize just how large the Mexican economy is, or how fast it is developing in world importance. In fact, if asked to name the G20, the likelihood is that Mexico would come well down on a person's list, if, indeed, it appeared at all.

But with an economy measured in trillions of dollars, Mexico happens to be the world's 11th largest. It's also a great export market for American companies. Cross border trade between the US and Mexico reached around $507 billion in 2013, and is still growing. This is not surprising, as Mexico not only has a large population – at 120 million it is the largest Hispanic country by numbers in the world – but a young and vibrant workforce. Indeed, at more than 51 million, Mexico has the 13th largest workforce in the world (and an unemployment rate less than 5%).

The median age in Mexico is 27½, just around the age that financial management begins to turn to real consumer spending. Half of Mexico's inhabitants are considered to be middle class, and only 7% are over 65 years old (though life expectancy is 77). It's easy to see that a major portion of the population is in the home growing and expenditure increasing mode of life.

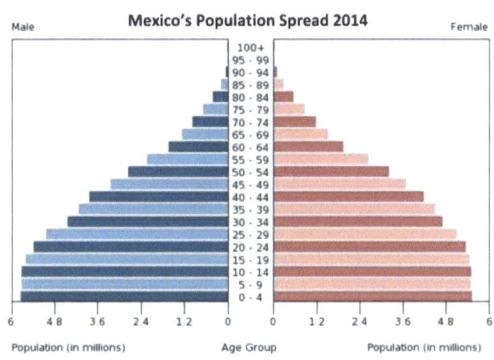

And the good news doesn't stop there. The Mexican government is putting in place programs aimed at catapulting the nation to one of the World's best educated. Children and young adults are being encouraged to stay in education longer and the number of graduates these policies are producing continues to balloon.

Many people think of Mexico as a largely agricultural, pseudo third world country, but that couldn't be further from the truth. It has a rapidly growing consumer base, a social system that is encouraging an explosion in education and has already led to an 86% literacy rate amongst teenagers, and a diverse and growing economy. More than 90% of its trade is conducted under free trade agreements with more than 50 countries

Mexico's industrial base accounts for 37% of its economy, whereas agriculture counts makes up less than 4%. The services sector in Mexico supplies the remainder of its national product, a percentage that is likely to continue to expand.

All these are reasons for American exporters to be bullish about the prospects for business with Mexico, but the good news still doesn't stop there.

A growing economy

Mexico was hit hard by the financial crisis of 2008, and saw the size of its economy shrink by a massive 6.2% in 2009 as a result. But the government took sizeable and swift measures, and has managed the economy well since. Consequently the bounce-back has been a marked one.

In 2010, GDP grew by 5.4%, and this was followed by a further upturn of 4% in its economy in 2011, then 3.6% in 2012. This rate of growth dipped to 1.4% in 2013, the IMF estimated 2014 growth had recovered to 2.1% in 2014, and, in its latest report (December 2014) expects the Mexican economy to grow by 3.2% and 3.5% in 2015 and 2016 respectively – the fastest of all Latin American countries and faster than the European Union and the USA (in 2016).

In a global economy that is struggling, Mexico's future looks far brighter than most.

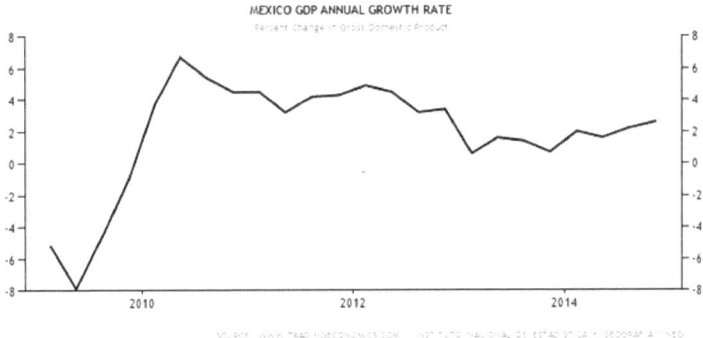

And Mexico has plenty of room to continue this level of economic activity for years to come. We've already seen the potential incumbent in its population, but the policies and economic management of its government shouldn't be underestimated. It spent heavily to turn around the economy from the dark days of 2009, and yet its budget deficit is only 2.5% of its GDP. Its net public debt is just 37.7% of GDP. Compare these numbers to the United States' budget deficit of around 8.25% of GDP and net debt of over 70% of GDP.

With an unemployment rate of just 4.9%, a diverse economy leaning heavily toward the service sector, and a young population whose consumer mentality is growing along with its level of education, and it's easy to see that Mexico is a market place that looks set to suck in exports from the United States for many years.

And this is good news for those companies looking to export to Mexico or open up franchise opportunities in the country. Each day, approximately $1.25 billion of goods and services crosses between the two neighbors. The country is considered so important to the fortunes of American business that businesses have invested over $150 billion in Mexico since the turn of the Millennium.

Mexican growth to be fueled further?

Another driver of growth in Mexico will be the energy market, undergoing a period of massive reform. Over the last twelve months or so, new legislation has opened the market to American companies. Mexico is estimated to have more than 110 billion barrels of oil resources, and it seems likely that NAFTA agreements are going to be rewritten to remove exclusions that had previously existed under the agreement.

It seems likely that US companies will seek to expand their oil and gas exploration activities deeper into Mexico. Indeed, several agreements have already been signed, such as the purchase of a majority stake in Fermaca (Mexico's leading provider of gas transportation infrastructure) by Partners Group. More American expansion is likely, including in the provision of offshore support vessels. Mexican law prohibits such operations to be conducted by non-Mexican companies, but with the relaxation of the market and other regulations, US companies are already discussing joint ventures with their Mexican counterparts.

There is likely to be more oil produced in Mexico, but also rapid growth of cheaper imports. Electricity generators south of the border are already beginning to invest in pipelines which will transport cheap oil into Mexico from the United States, and with the recent fall in the oil price the Mexican consumer could get a further boost which could add billions to its GDP over the coming years.

If you're not yet convinced of the opportunity that Mexico represents for your franchise business, then perhaps we should compare it to another popular export destination, and one that is not only in vogue but considered by many to be the savior of American business.

China or Mexico: the choice is yours

China is now World's largest economy, and as it has been moving toward a more capitalist and consumer driven society it has been growing rapidly. But the IMF predicts a rapid slowdown in its rate of growth over the coming years, and this will affect its ability to grow its imports.

Whilst discussing China's imports – and remembering that what really interests us is US exports into China – it's worth noting the size of the market for US companies. And here we're not considering the size of the population, but the actual real cash market. The reasons for examining it this way will become obvious over the next couple of paragraphs.

In 2014, US companies exported $124 billion of goods and services to China. Compare this number to the $240 billion of exports to Mexico (www.census.gov).

Perhaps revisiting Mexico's economic make-up will help explain further the advantage of targeting Mexico rather than China.

Mexico's economy is leaned toward the service sector. Though industry is a large contributor to GDP, and a large employer, increasingly Mexico is reliant on imported finished goods. The main exports to Mexico from the US include mechanical machinery, electronic and electrical equipment, motor parts, fuels and oils, and plastics. Add into this mix consumer products and foodstuffs, and you begin to get some idea of the importance that Mexico places upon its business links and imports from the United States.

China, on the other hand, is a mainly industrial nation. It buys raw materials and then produces goods to sell domestically and for the export market. The Chinese may be looking to ignite its consumer, but this will be for the benefit of its own industries and not for rapid growth of its import market. To put this in perspective, in the $124 billion of goods and services exported by the US to China is dwarfed by the $466 billion of goods and services imported.

But it's not just this systemic difference that makes Mexico a more attractive proposition for companies that want to increase profits through exports. Geographically, Mexico is a far easier target.

Mexico: a single border

Mexico and the United States share a common 2,000 mile border. But they also share policing, transportation, environmental, and telecommunications responsibilities and duties. In 2010, Presidents Obama and Calderon created the Steering Committee for 21st Century Border Management, and there are initiatives between the two countries to promote trade, the major one being the North American Free Trade Agreement (NAFTA).

As yet, there are few such agreements and pacts between the United States and China. But there is a huge distance, over water.

It is easier to transport goods to Mexico, by road or rail, and the trade agreements between the two countries have fostered even closer trade and cultural ties. Even though a large proportion of the country is Spanish speaking, increasing education and a population of over 1 million United States' expats are changing this rapidly.

What all this means for the franchise opportunity

Okay, so we've seen that Mexico is a large country, with a young, vibrant population, and that its economy is dominated by services and consumerism. Its growth prospects are second to none, and its links to the United States are unparalleled. But how does this translate to the franchise opportunity?

Franchising is one of the powerhouse sectors of the Mexican economy. It is growing at an incredible rate of **around 10% per year**, and, according to research consultants Feher & Feher, Mexico is one of the world's top ten franchise developers.

The market is supported by a strong legal framework, with more than 1500 brands currently franchised through over 75,000 points of sale. Around 900,000 people are employed by franchises market in Mexico. The majority of these franchises are originated in the United States, though around 80% are Mexican brands.

The legal framework under which the Mexican franchise market works is closely related to branding and trademark laws, and is promoted by the National Franchise Program (PNF). This program promotes investment in franchise concepts, with the goal of increasing employment in the sector. In conjunction with the Ministry of the Economy and the Mexican Franchise Association, the PNF provides opportunities to Mexican entrepreneurs to create or re-engineer franchise opportunities: this includes providing support to investors looking to acquire international franchise concepts.

Ideal Franchise Products/ Opportunities

The food and restaurant sector has always been a profitable and popular franchise model in Mexico, although the services sector is now growing rapidly, too. In particular, home care services and entertainment concepts for children are growing strongly, as are home improvement, business services, and the hospitality sector.

US brands and products are readily accepted by the Mexican consumer, and it is expected that franchise opportunities will continue to be in demand in the coming years as investors seek to innovate in secondary markets.

All in all, a great place to export to: but not without difficulties

So, Mexico has a strong and growing economy and great trade links with the United States. Its business and economic environment is more conducive to exporting US companies than China is, and transportation links are in place and easy to negotiate. And yet US companies often under estimate the franchise opportunity just over the border, or consider it to be riddled with legalities that cause more cost and concern than end profit.

It's certainly true that there are administrative and legal issues to deal with. Goods have to be properly classified, and valued for tax purposes. They have to be accompanied by complete NAFTA certificates (if NAFTA originated), and exportation documentation can be more than a little problematic.

There are horror stories of even the largest US companies falling foul of the Mexican importation process, and perhaps it is these that cause such pessimism among would-be exporters and franchisors. And that's why using the right Mexperts is a must: someone who has the contacts, experience, and knowledge to ensure your exports clear customs and reach your customer promptly and without unnecessary cost to you.

Chapter 2

HISTORY IS ON YOUR SIDE

Ok, now a history lesson that they are probably not teaching in public schools or universities. It's not only the current economy that beckons the franchisor. Just like an investor who wants to see the background and history behind an investment before he commits to it, so too do franchising and exporting businesses. And in this regard, Mexico is better placed than almost any other target export market of the United States. Relationships have always been close – even if sometimes a little taut – between the two nations. But trade relations really began to take off in the early 1990's, with the introduction of NAFTA.

NAFTA – A brief history

The North American Free Trade Agreement (NAFTA) was signed by the US President, George Bush, The Mexican President, Salinas, and the Canadian Prime Minister, Brian Mulroney, in 1992. It was ratified by all three countries' legislatures in 1993, and came into force on January 1, 1994. It created the world's largest free trade zone, and has reduced the costs of trading, increased business investment, and increased global competitiveness.

But it wasn't Bush who first considered the importance of such a free trade zone, and nor was it President Clinton, even though it is considered as one of his first successes. The whole concept actually began with President Ronald Reagan, after Congress passed the Trade and Tariff Act in 1984. It was this Act that allowed the President to negotiate free trade agreements and cancelled the ability for Congress to change any of the negotiating points. Reagan could see how successful the European Union's continent wide free trade agreement had become, and set himself the goal of creating similar on this side of the Atlantic.

His first step was the Canada-US Free Trade Agreement in 1988, the success of which prompted President Bush to begin negotiations with Mexico to achieve similar. One of the main aims was to level the playing field between import and export tariffs: prior to NAFTA, Mexican tariffs on US imports were 250% higher than US tariffs on Mexican imports. With these negotiations under way, Canada requested a trilateral agreement, and this led to the signing of NAFTA into the laws of all three countries.

NAFTA brings advantages...

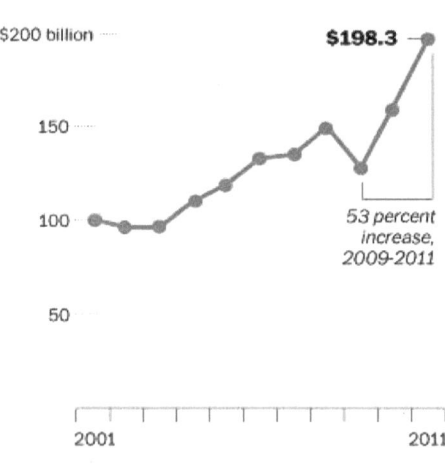

$200 billion

$198.3

150

100

53 percent increase, 2009-2011

50

2001   2011

In less than less than 20 years, NAFTA has helped to see trade between the three member countries more than quintuple. In 1993, trade between the United States, Canada, and Mexico stood at a little under $300 million. By 2011 this had grown to over $1.7 trillion. US exports have grown to more than $450 billion, nearly half of which were to Mexico (see chart).

Low cost imports into the United States have also grown, to over $570 billion. Mexican oil exports to the United States benefited from the removal of tariffs, which has helped keep fuel prices in the United States lower than they would otherwise have been.

US farm exports have been one of the main beneficiaries, with lower Mexican tariffs encouraging growth of more than 150%.

...but it also has some disadvantages

Ross Perot, in 1992, said that he believed NAFTA would cost millions of Americans their jobs. In fact, he predicted that 5 million jobs would be lost to Mexico. This, of course, has not been the case, though there has been some migration of companies, and therefore jobs, to the Mexico's lower labor cost base. This may also have helped keep wage inflation subdued in the United States – the threat of companies moving factories and production capacity to Mexico is seen by Unions and workers as a very real one.

But the effect on jobs was not a one way street. Agriculture suffered in Mexico as cheap American imports from subsidized US farming corporations hurt producers. With US businesses setting up shop in Mexico, the Union movement and subsequently Mexican labor laws have been strengthened. Prior to NAFTA, Mexican workers had no labor rights or health protection. Now, more than a third of its workforce is in the 'maquiladora' program that gives such rights and protection.

NAFTA: Benefits explodes trade

The elimination of expensive tariffs has helped to reduce American inflation by decreasing the cost of imports. This has helped usher in an unprecedented period of low interest rates, which has helped homebuyers with lower mortgage rates and also promoted retail businesses.

For businesses, agreements on rights for business investors has helped reduce the cost of trade, and this has been particularly good news for small businesses, where such costs have a far larger impact on margins.

Firms can now bid on cross border government contracts, and perhaps one of the most important by-products of NAFTA is the protection of intellectual property rights cross border.

Those politicians that have argued the demerits of NAFTA, and especially those that have called for its abolishment due to the effect on US jobs have largely been proved wrong. Hilary Clinton and Barrack Obama have both attacked NAFTA. Clinton promised to strictly enforce all trade agreements and either amend or back out of NAFTA. Obama said it helped businesses at the expense of workers in the United States. Ron Paul, during the 2008 Presidential election campaign, said that he would abolish it, a position he maintained in his 2012 campaign. Going against the grain was Republican John McCain, who said he supported all free trade agreements as being ultimately good for the economy. So, who is right?

It may be a bit of both. Certainly, some industries, such as automobiles, textiles, computers, and electrical equipment manufacturers have seen jobs lost to more competitive Mexican factory-workers. This has also had an effect on wage inflation in the United States.

However, the flipside is that price inflation and interest rates have been lower than they would otherwise have been.

NAFTA has seen an explosion of trade between the three member countries, and exports from the US to Mexico and Canada have ballooned, more than trebling during the course of NAFTA.

One of the main beneficiaries has been the farming industry, which has seen exports to Mexico and Canada grow by well, over 150%. And this growth compares to export growth to the rest of the world of just 65% during the same period. Mexico is now the top destination for US exports of beef, soybean meal, corn sweeteners, apples, and beans, and the second largest for corn, soybeans, and oils. And franchise businesses in the food sector are benefiting from this super growth and lower cost of quality produce.

The US service industry has also seen a huge payday. With over 40% of the American economy set in the service sector, being able to easily transport them to Mexico and Canada saw such exports grow from just $25 billion in 1993 to over $105 billion in 2007, before the financial crisis hit: imports of such services from Canada and Mexico is less than $40 billion.

It's not just cheaper tariffs that have helped US inflation remain low. Imports of oil from Mexico have more than replaced imports of oil from Iran, and this in turn has helped America with cheaper fuel costs. And the elimination of food price tariffs has reduced food costs, too.

Americans have always invested abroad. But since NAFTA, US investment in Mexico has increased at a massive pace (and vice versa). In fact, by 2012 (latest figures) US direct investment in Mexico had reached over $101 billion, and is increasing at around $14 billion per year. That is investment into manufacturing, finance, and banking services, and is now set to be further boosted by investment into the oil industry. And that has been tremendous news for American businesses, which are using Mexico as a powerhouse for expansion.

No truck with moving goods

As you will see as you get to know me, I have no problem bashing both political parties on both sides of the border. Here is a story that really will blow your mind about NAFTA.

NAFTA's main aim is to increase trade in the North American zone, between Canada, the United States, and Mexico. And it has really been successful, as we have already seen. But for the success to be made really permanent, then there has to be a freedom not just of trade, but movement of goods, too: in other words, a breaking down of all trade barriers.

So NAFTA requires that each country signing up to it gives foreign service-providers 'treatment no less favorable' than she gives her own nationals. You would think that this would mean Mexican and

Canadian trucks could take product across the border and deliver to importers.

So, Clinton signed agreements for Mexican trucks to cross the border and ply their import deliveries to the USA. But the Teamsters weren't happy about this. The trouble is that Mexican truck drivers are paid about half of what US drivers are paid. The Teamsters argued that Mexican trucking companies would be coming over in their thousands and taking American truckers' jobs. They said that Mexican trucks and truckers were unsafe. So they lobbied congress. Newt Gingrich had even said he expects 150,000 Mexican trucks to cross the border as soon as the restrictions are lifted.

Because of this lobbying, Obama put a stop to all of Clinton's plans with regard to Mexican trucks: Mexican trucks were restricted in the US on safety grounds. That was a few years ago, and it unleashed a fair amount of mayhem.

Mexico wasn't about to sit down and take this action on the chin. They fought back, slapping a whole raft of tariffs on US imports. But its government didn't announce a lead in period, or a period of reflection and time for dialogue and discussion. They announced the new duties and taxes, and they came into effect within seven days of the announcement.

Now, at that time, and while all this was going on, we had arranged for 36 trucks to haul 800 tons of cheese from Wisconsin to Mexico for one of our clients. Each truck cost $3200. When the cheese was on the road, the taxes came into force. With 25% tax suddenly imposed upon the produce, the export to Mexico suddenly became worthless: the cheese was never going to sell.

There was nothing our client could do, but to recall the cheese and waste it. Their orders to their suppliers were cancelled. Trucking contracts were cancelled. The company lost money, truckers found themselves without work, farmers and producers lost jobs. The very thing that the Teamsters said they were protecting, the situation that Obama created, cost US jobs and profits. And that was just a tiny microcosm of what happened, with one exporter out of tens of thousands affected.

Fortunately common sense has prevailed, and, after new agreements were signed last year, earlier this year Mexican trucks have been allowed to apply for licenses to cross the border.

Chapter 3

YOUR BRAND IS YOUR TRADEMARK

Trademarks in Mexico – the law

Mexico is now part of the Madrid Protocol, which allows simultaneous registration of trademarks in several countries added to the Madrid Protocol. Once registered a trademark remains registered for a period of ten years and is automatically renewable for same period by paying fees for renewal.

A trademark can be practically anything, including words, symbols, logos, and designs, as well as trade names, and three dimensional goods that are distinctive of a trademarks; designs are protected under other forms of protection named Industrial Designs at IMPI.

The trademark needs to be registered at WIPO office designating to Mexico as country of protection, then WIPO notifies to IMPI (Mexican Trademark Office) that was registered a trademark under Madrid Protocol and once this is done it is then best to arrange protection with the Mexican Customs Border Authority. This will stop counterfeit goods at the border, protecting your business is Mexico and the US. MSME can arrange this protection for you.

Have you already trademarked your brand in Mexico? If not it could already be too late.

Don't be chicken to develop Mexico

This is the story of El Pollo Loco, now a successful American grilled chicken chain, but which had been first developed in Mexico. The rights to develop the brand in Mexico had been given to El Pollo Loco Inc in 1996, including all the trademarks.

The Mexican founder had agreed with the American company that it would take the concept and grow it in Mexico, with a ten-year agreement signed and sealed. Trade secrets, methods, designs, and other confidential information were disclosed. The American company was found to have taken all this information and, quite literally, used it for its own means in the United States while letting the Mexican opportunity slide.

The result was that the franchise in Mexico was copied, with imitators taking over to such an extent that the competitive edge which El Pollo Loco had was decimated. By 2004, the grilled chicken market in Mexico – now worth hundreds of millions of dollars – was dominated by these imitators, and the Mexican arm sued the American company. In 2007, the courts in California found in favor of the Mexican company and awarded it more than $22 million.

It goes to show how big an opportunity Mexico is for franchise businesses, but also how important it is to have someone on the ground protecting interests.

What is a trademark?

A trademark shows the source of the goods and services and, in the case of a franchised business, allows the consumer to distinguish between similar offerings. It's a mark of the quality of a business and its product. It helps a customer quickly identify other goods made by the same manufacturer, services offered by the same company, and both offered by franchisees. The business of a franchisee, just as the product of a manufacturer, has its reputation associated with its brand (trademark) – and this directly affects sales. A trademark can tell current and prospective customers all about the history, quality, and even the origin of a franchised business.

A trademark is also about the goodwill that a franchisor has built up. This directly affects the price at which a company can franchise and that franchisees can sell their produce. Goodwill is like the reputation of a company: and we all know that a good reputation takes years to build, but minutes to destroy.

When a product or franchise is traded by the use of a copied trademark – so called parallel selling – the expectations that have been built up within the consumer can be destroyed. Quality and value are likely to be missing, because of the factors of customer satisfaction that may be affected:

- No after sales service

- No guarantees honored

- Packaging and instructions in poor language

- Poor instructions

- Reusability and recyclability inaccuracies on packaging

- Health information or nutritional value mis-advice

Not only will the good name of the franchise be affected, but also its product sales, both now and in the future. And don't think that just because a trademark (or franchise) is registered and protected in the United States that it will be protected in Mexico. Some of the largest companies have fallen foul of this misconception, will be seen in a short while.

Make sure your Apple isn't poisoned

 In early November 2012, Apple Inc lost a trademark battle in Mexico. The case had started in 2009, and involves its US and (almost) worldwide trademark, iPhone. You see, unbeknown to Apple, when it began to market its key product in Mexico in 2007 there was already a company called iFone trading in the country.

The Mexican telecoms company, iFone, had been trading under its name for four years before Apple started to market its iPhone product in Mexico. In 2009, iFone filed a lawsuit claiming trademark infringement against the US

corporate giant, saying that the similar names caused confusion to its customers and consumers in Mexico.

Now it would appear that Apple will need to compensate iFone for the use of the iPhone name.

What this story demonstrates is the strength of the copyright law in Mexico: if a company's trademark is registered in Mexico, no matter how big a company comes along with its own product the original will be protected in law.

Properly registering your trademark in Mexico will mean you can take a bite of the business apple without fear of it being poisoned against you.

The IMPI

The IMPI is the public agency that manages all industrial trademarks in Mexico, and as such application for trademark registration has to be made to it.

For any trademark applicant who is not resident in Mexico, a power of attorney must be given to handle the application for trademark registration and protection. The POA must be signed in the presence of two witnesses, and it must also state that the person signing on behalf of the company wanting to apply for trademark registration has the authority to do so.

If the applicant is not identical to the holder of the internationally recognized trademark supporting the application, then papers of assignment of the trademark to the applicant will also need to be furnished with the application forms.

Payment of all fees must be made with the application, and these payments cover the filing fee, and trademark examination fees. This fee has to be paid in Mexican Pesos and be submitted with his application.

This may sound a complex and drawn out process (it can take several months to move from application to registration). It may be that the need to complete application forms in Spanish fills you with dread. But it's certain that your business will benefit from trademark protection, and suffer without it. It's the first thing you must do before selling in Mexico.

Resources:

Here are the links to the Mexican Institute of Industrial Property (Instituto Mexicano de Propiedad Industrial, or IMPI) and Mexican Government Trademark Search Engine:

Mexico Patent and Trademark Office (IMPI)

http://www.impi.gob.mx/

Mexican Government Search Engine for Trademarks

http://marcanet.impi.gob.mx/marcanet/controler/home

Of course, doing business in Mexico and accessing a market with tens of millions of potential customers doesn't end with trademark registration. Your products also have to be labeled correctly, and if they're not…well, let's see what happened to Wal-Mart when its labels failed to meet Mexican legal requirements.

Chapter 4

TRADEMARKS IDENTIFY, LABELS EXPLAIN

Don't think that because you have properly registered your franchise in the United States that it will be immune from attack in Mexico. The trademark laws may be less relevant for service businesses, but if your franchise business is selling goods and products then you had better make certain that you have taken all necessary precautions to protect your business.

We've already seen how franchise businesses that fail to keep on top of their game in Mexico can quickly become copied, and how even the largest companies can have lose trademark lawsuits. Here's a story that describes another problem that unprepared American companies face when trading in Mexico.

In 2007/ 8 Wal-Mart was well and truly riding the wave of the Mexican retail revolution promoted by NAFTA. It was opening new stores almost on a weekly basis, and sales were rocketing. Everything was rosy in the Wal-Mart garden, and it was exporting huge amounts of stock across the border. This was, perhaps, the perfect example of how NAFTA could provide success for all: an American retailer, with store locations in Mexico employing Mexican people and selling goods made by American suppliers and exported from the United States to Mexico. A trade zone working in perfect harmony.

But trouble was brewing.

Wal-Mart failed to change many of its labels to display product information in Spanish. And the Spanish authorities didn't like that. Wal-Mart claimed that it was a computer glitch that had caused the mistake, and then blamed human error. Whatever the problem was, the Mexican authorities didn't take kindly to Wal-Mart's protestations. They told Wal-Mart to change its labels. And then they shut down the Mexico City store until Wal-Mart complied with the order.

Wal-Mart: not just America's biggest retailer, but the largest in the world. According to the Fortune Global 500 list, in 2012 Wal-Mart is the world's third largest public corporation, employing over 2 million people in more than 8500 stores around the globe. And yet a company of this size and stature made a basic error: it failed to act on legal requirements and advice, or, perhaps, it just didn't realize what the rules of exportation were.

And these labeling rules can be quite complex and hidden away within the wording of NOM51

Welcome to NOM51, a law that makes everything clearer!

The requirements for labeling products in preparation for export can be very complex, particularly for food products and nutritional supplements. Fortunately all the details are contained within the appropriate laws, including NOM51. Unfortunately, as with many laws, NOM51 is subject to ad hoc amendments that are designed to keep the law up-to-date with modern practice. Further, the law and amendments are written in Spanish.

At a minimum, product labels must be in Spanish. These labels must be on the product when they are imported into Mexico, and if they aren't then the import will be stopped at the border and held. There may be exemptions, but these are few and far between and have to be arranged months in advance with labels provided for affixing within Mexico.

Typically, products must be labeled with the following information:

- Product name

- Quantity or amount

- Name, registration number and address of the producer

- Name, registration number and address of the importer

- Country of origin (and there are special rules here)

- Relevant warnings

- Instructions, or reference to an instruction manual, if appropriate

There are laws that cover labeling requirements for textiles, pre-package foods and non-alcoholic beverages, and then further laws to cover other consumer products not covered by other laws!

Certain goods, such as silver-plated products, leather goods and clothing have one set of labeling rules, whilst other textiles and apparel have to comply with a separate set of requirements.

Under NOM51, food and non-alcoholic beverages also have to include:

- Expiration date

- Storage instructions

- Preparation and use instructions

Again, all of this must be in Spanish.

Common mistakes are made time and again

Wal-Mart's experience was a big case at the time, and served to highlight the problems of non-translated labeling. Yet still many exports from the United States to Mexico are held up at the border, or even confiscated never to be seen again, because labeling is in English.

Many companies also believe that a straight translation on current US product labeling, from English to Spanish, will suffice. But this is not the case, as there are additional items of information needed on product labels to comply with not just import labeling requirements but general labeling requirements.

Common mistakes are often made because exporters try to cut corners, using the in-house expertise of employees who only have the time resource to work part time on an area of competence that requires full time maintenance. As Wal-Mart discovered, a few dollars saved on the US side of the border can cost millions in Mexico.

Resources:

NOM 51 Requirements

http://dof.gob.mx/nota_detalle.php?codigo=5137518&fecha=05/04/2010

Now you have your trademark registered and protected, and your products are labeled correctly for the Mexican market, you can start exporting, right? Well, you're not quite there yet. Before your products leave on their way to the importer, you need to make sure that you, or your customers in Mexico, won't be paying unnecessary taxes. Doing so means you need to understand product classification.

Chapter 5

CLASSIFY YOUR PRODUCT – IT'S YOUR DUTY

As with trademarking, there are also rules when classifying your products within Mexico and for import. Again, this is less required for service franchises, but if you are selling products in any shape and form then you'll need to know and observe the classification laws.

To demonstrate the importance of product classification, I'd like to take you back to when I first started exporting to Mexico and was a big lesson that I teach everyone, you need to know your HS number, because no one else cares. I began my career as an export manager for my family's nationwide pizza distribution company, Roma Food (www.romafood.com). My job was to travel around Mexico and convince distributors to buy our many products including flour to make pizza. At the time, we sold to Mexico, not in Mexico. So our delivery was to the border, and the importer/distributor took care of everything else. After a while we had several distributors as customers around Mexico, using different import agencies to manage the trade of goods between us and the importers. Talking to one of my distributors, I discovered that he had been paying a 5% import duty on the flour for many years. While speaking to my other distributors, I found out they were not paying the 5% duty on the flour.

Needless to say, my distributor was more than a little upset when he was told that the flour he had been buying from us should have no duty applied to it. For years it had been paying its 5%, meaning its margins were lower and costs higher, when it should have paid nothing. It may even have been that sales had been lost because of a lack of competitiveness in pricing. The cost to the distributor amounted to thousands of dollars and all because his import agency misclassified the flour product. The agency classified it as all purpose flour, when in fact it was special flour for pizza with certain characteristics. I learned the lesson then, that most agencies are lazy and do not care about which HS classification they assign, it is not their money. You need to know your HS Classification number.

What Are HS Classification Codes

Product classification codes are used to determine the rate and amount of duties and taxes that have to be paid on imported goods. The Harmonized Commodity Description and Coding System (HS) is recognized around the world as a standardized system of names and numbers for classifying traded products. It has been developed and is maintained by the World Customs Organization (WCO).

The WCO sets these numbers, and countries are obliged to use them. However, though tariff schedules are based upon HS, countries will set their own rates of duties.

The system allows exporting and importing nations to keep track of trade, and monitor and collect taxes. The tax collecting part of the process is undertaken by customs authorities, and higher duties are levied on the goods that are in competition with internal manufacturers that produce the same or similar goods. If there is no competitive product made within a country's borders, then duties can't be levied.

Some goods won't need an import permit, whilst others will. The classification process is part of the overall framework that enables the correct identification of those goods that require a permit as against those that don't. Incorrect classification could mean unnecessary time and effort applying for import permits, as well as the financial implications of wrongly taxed goods.

Importing products to Mexico is only viable if the cost of doing so is not so outside the realms of competitiveness. Whilst retail taxes are levied on all goods, import duties are there to protect domestic business, the idea being that they will bring the cost of imported goods into line with domestic goods and negate competitive advantage on price only.

Goods that are misclassified could have import duties applied that are above the legal requirement. Not only will this harm price competitiveness, but will incur charges that cannot later be reclaimed.

For goods to clear border customs authorities, importation and exportation documentation must match, and this includes the HS number. Mismatching will mean goods getting stuck at the border, incurring further costs and delays on their way to point of sale.

Classification of goods is a complicated process, and requires attention to detail. For example, the simple task of classifying an oven for export/ import needs confirmation of the type of oven it is – gas, electric, etc. – and the use of the oven – domestic or industrial. In other words, goods have to be classified as to their form and their function.

NAFTA and HS

US products either have minimal duties or are exempted from duties altogether when imported into Mexico. However, the rules of origin are stringent. This ensures that the goods are indeed US produced, and not manufactured elsewhere before final export to Mexico.

Under NAFTA, a Certificate of Origin must be signed by the exporter. Although an exporter who is not a producer of goods can request the producer to provide the certificate for him, but the obligation to do so remains with the exporter.

The exporter must pass the Certificate of Origin to the importer, and this will then be presented to Customs to in order to qualify for preferential rates of importation duties. Where the product doesn't qualify for NAFTA tariff preferences, then the Certificate must not be completed as the import may qualify for other preferential treatment under the Most Favored Nation (MFN) tariff rates.

The NAFTA rules of origin are organized to coincide with the HS, and the first step to take to assess qualification for preferential importation duties is to determine the correct HS number.

After this has been determined, then the appropriate tariff can be assessed. If the MFN rate is zero, then no NAFTA certificate is required. If the MFN rate is not zero, then the HS number should be used to locate the applicable rule of origin under NAFTA, and determination of the NAFTA rate can be made.

The Certificate of Origin

 The Certificate of Origin requires the names and addresses of exporters, producers, and importers, as well as a full description of goods, relevant HS numbers, costs, and declaration of origin, and must be filled in if the goods being exported, or likely to be exported during a 'blanket period' of up to one year, exceeds $1000 in value.

Producer Name

The first and last name of the producer of the goods must be provided, and included with the company name of the producer (if applicable).

Tariff Code

The Tariff Code is the product specific HS number, and will be between 6 and 10 digits.

Exporter/ Shipper of Goods

It has to be stipulated if the shipper is the producer, and if not then if the goods qualify as originating goods, the level of reliance on the producer that the goods qualify as originating goods, or the completed and signed Certificate of Origin provided to the exporter by the producer.

Avoid the common mistakes, and use the Mexperts

Even experienced exporters and importers, and multi-national companies get their HS codes wrong and incorrectly complete

Certificates of Origin. Sometimes, as in the case of the pizza products company highlighted earlier, misclassified goods manage to cross the border for years. And it's never the goods that are misclassified with a lower than required tariff.

Misclassification will cost time, goodwill, and, perhaps most importantly, money. It can mean products crossing the border becoming uncompetitive in your target market.

Resources:

The Census Bureau has a simple-to-use free tool at their website and a short instructional video that shows you how to find the exact 10 digit code you need. Here's the handy link:

Schedule B Search Engine

https://uscensus.prod.3ceonline.com/

The Bottom Line

As you can probably see, I'm very passionate about doing business in Mexico. I think that there are plenty of great companies in the United States that are really missing out on a great opportunity by ignoring the market just across the border. I've helped small companies get big by taking them to Mexico.

A growing market waits for you, and the reason I wrote this book is so that you, too, can see the huge potential that is Mexico. I hope that I've helped you: hopefully you've learned a lot, and now have the tools to start out on the exciting journey to exporting your product to Mexico.

Of course, this book only deals with the beginning of your journey. Once you've started on your journey, then you'll also need to fully understand the intricacies of franchising, marketing and selling in Mexico, and how to reach out to prospective franchisees, and distributors. And after you've done that, then the execution of your franchise strategy, delivering products and logistics.

My book, **The 3 Things You Need to Know Before You Begin Franchising in Mexico.** Will explain all you need to know to become a Mexpert, like me and my colleagues at MFME. Or, perhaps, you'd like to speak to us direct? Why not visit the MFME website, www.mexicofranchisingmadeeasy.com for more information about us and the book that will help your business prosper?

Guest Chapter

Chris Martinez - Website En 5 Dias

WHAT IF YOU COULD GO BACK IN TIME?

"I wish I could go back 15 years ago to when everything online was so much less competitive and so much cheaper"

Zach Linford - Conversion Optimization Specialist

In January 2015, renowned Conversion Optimization Specialist Zach Linford said how he wished he could go back in time to the early 2000s when the world of online marketing was in its infancy and profiting was so much easier and less competitive.

In this chapter, you will learn how the opportunity to make money online easily, just as it was at the turn of the century, is possible with the proper guidance in Mexico.

The U.S Online in 2000

Let's start by looking at the United States as it was in the year 2000. At that time, there were rougly281 Million people living in the U.S., with an Average Household Income of $42,148, and the Average Cost of Home was around $119,600.

From an online perspective 43.1% of Americans had access to the internet and Google launched Google Adwords connecting advertisers with consumers for as little as 5-10 cents per **click**.

For those that adapted quickly to this new technology, they were able to make millions of dollars and build massive fortunes virtually on demand. At this time, if you simply put up a website and start driving traffic you could amass countless leads and sales with very little effort.

The U.S Online in 2015

Now let's look at the U.S. online landscape in 2015. Currently there are approximately 319 Million people living in the U.S., the

Average Household Income is around $50,500 annually, and the Average Cost of Home is $178,500.

Since 2000, we've seen a dramatic adoption of the internet and currently 86.7% of Americans have access to the internet. With that increase in users, Google AdWords costs have also increased from anywhere between 2-$300 per click.

So we ask you the questions....

Knowing What You Know Now...

"What would you do to go back in time and grow your business online all over again?"

Would you embrace the digital technology quicker? Would you shift your focus to generating passive ecommerce that requires little to no sales personnel? Would you fast track your social media department to capture engagement on sites like Facebook and Twitter?

For most businesses, they would answer "Yes" to all of these things because at now each one has been proven to drive revenue and market share.

Mexico Online in 2015

It's time to look at the present state of the online world in Mexico. While some of the numbers might seem different compared to the U.S. today, the relevance is striking. To date, there are approximately 122 Million people living in Mexico, with an Average Household Income $9,747 U.S. annually ($146,205 pesos), and the Average Purchase Price of a Home is around $38,438 U.S. ($576,570 pesos).

The most striking number is that 43.5% of Mexicans have access to the internet (5.3 Million people) which is almost exactly similar to the internet access statistics of Americans in the year 2000. Furthermore, in 2015 Mexico will become 8th Largest Country for Internet Usage surpassing Germany.

Mexico is also adapting to mobile internet technology faster than almost any country in the Americas. For example, in 2012 of the people who had access to the internet only 34% of those Mexicans could access the internet via a mobile device. However by 2013 that numbered nearly DOUBLED to 64% in just one year.

Social Media: US vs Mexico

Social Media also plays a major role in the daily online usage much more so than here in the United States. Not only is the Mexican culture driven more by social engagement, but the growth of the internet in Mexico has paralleled that of Facebook, unlike in the U.S. how our internet growth has paralleled Google.

Simply put, in the US when we think about the internet we think of Google. For example, if someone asks you a question and you don't know the answer, you would normally just respond with "Google it. However, in Mexico when they think about the internet they immediately think of FACEBOOK so it's imperative that American brands understand the significance of the Facebook presence and how it must be used to grow your market share and customer engagement.

In the United States, there are approximately 180 Million Facebook Users 18 years of age and older. In Mexico there are approximately 50 Million Facebook Users in Mexico 18 years and older. While there are over triple the users in the US, the percentage of internet users on Facebook in each respective country is astounding.

In the US, 67% of Internet Users in US have a Facebook account. In Mexico an amazing 92.5% of Internet Users have a Facebook account. In terms of usage, Mexico leads Latin America and potentially the world in the number of social media users in relation to overall internet users.

Furthermore, a recently study by ComScore shows that 45% of Social Media users in Mexico follow at least one brand and the main motivation for this is to take advantage of pricing discounts. Also 65% of Social Media users in the Mexico are under the age of 35, which means that capturing the younger generation of Mexicans can be achieved fairly easily through Facebook.

Top Facebook Pages

Below are a list of some of the top Facebook Pages in Mexico and if you look closer you'll notice that each of them is essentially an entertainment source for their followers. As a brand, if you can provide entertaining content for your followers, you stand to build a very loyal customer base through Facebook.

Wereverwero 17.9 Million Fans

Mana 16.6 Million Fans

Reik 16.1 Million Fans

Social Media: Mexico

Below is a list of social media graphs from ComScore that illustrate some of the opportunities for brands to engage with consumers in Mexico via Facebook and other social media platforms.

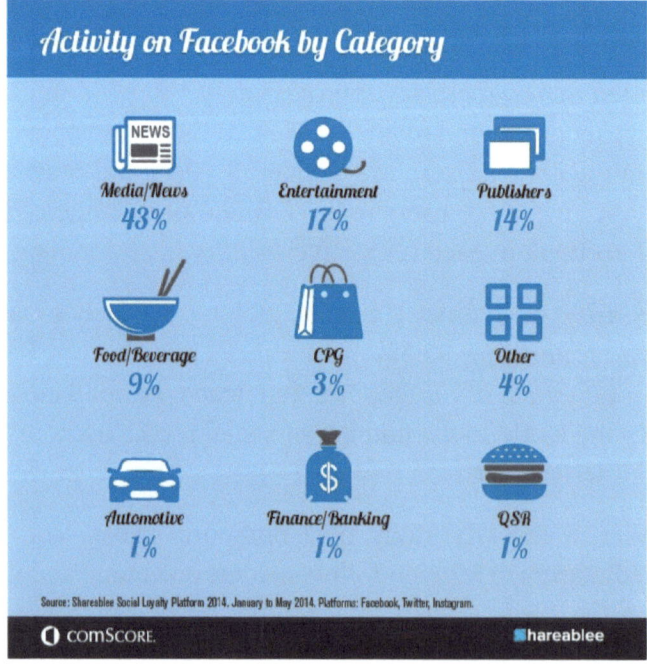

While the dominating focus of social media activity on Facebook in Mexico appears to be Media and Entertainment, the reason that Mexicans are not engaging with Brands and Retailers is because these companies are simply ignoring social media altogether. The existing companies in Mexico have failed to see the importance of social media and therefore they are not in the game. This gives an enormous opportunity to companies that aggressively embrace social media in Mexico.

How much is post type strategy affected by vertical in Mexico?

Post	Photo	Video	Status	Link
Entertainment	73.0%	3.2%	5.4%	18.3%
Media/News	39.4%	1.8%	2.6%	56.1%
Retail	87.1%	3.5%	5.0%	4.4%
Engagement				
Entertainment	76.5%	2.1%	0.9%	20.4%
Media/News	81.4%	0.4%	0.6%	17.5%
Retail	94.9%	1.5%	2.5%	1.0%

Source: Shareablee Social Loyalty Platform 2014. January to May 2014. Platforms: Facebook, Twitter, Instagram.

comSCORE.   hareablee

In this graphic you will see that social media engagement in Mexico is highly image-driven so integrating photos with your posts and advertisements is incredibly important. It also suggests that photo sharing platforms like Instagram and video sharing platforms like YouTube and Vine also can potentially be great growth opportunities in Mexico.

YouTube in Mexico

Online video consumption in Mexico is also growing at an exponential rate as individual personalities, who have until recently been ignored by mainstream media, are now gaining huge national following through YouTube. As these online video personalities start to gain an audience and create their own "channels", there are little or no brands endorsing these individuals or even advertising on their YouTube channels.

For example, the top YouTube Channel in Mexico in terms of view count is Werevertumorro with a total of 1.2 Billion views for all of their videos. While their videos are typically comical or satirical in nature, the sheer number of viewers makes this an excellent advertising opportunity for any brands.

While television advertising is still affordable by American standards, YouTube advertising on the popular Mexican channels is a much more cost-effective way to engage with the Mexican population and could yield better results.

Importance of Local Websites

When the internet started to explode in the United States in the early 2000s, it was not uncommon for a local business to show up organically anywhere throughout the country. However, as more people got online, marketers became more sophisticated, and IP address targeting advanced, Google began to focus more on connecting people with local businesses. This is why it is very rare for a business to have a strong organic presence across the nation.

The importance of having a local online presence in Mexico is imperative similarly to how it is in the US. Franchises should focus on building individual websites for each location so that it will be easier and more effective to market to those in that area. Customers, especially when searching on mobile, want to visit local businesses so each local business needs its own website.

This presents an enormous opportunity for local businesses since most businesses in Mexico still do not have a website. Whereas in the US nearly every industry has become extremely competitive, the online landscape in Mexico is untapped. With the right approach, a local business can dominate the online market and own the local market.

Take for example the story of Hector Bravo. In the United States, "plumbing" is one of the most competitive industries online. It can sometimes take $20k and over a year to show up on the first page of Google for the word "plumber (enter your city name)" if you're a local business. But this is not the case in Mexico at the current moment.

If you are to go into Google and type in "Fontanero Guadalajara" (Fontanero is Spanish for "plumber"), then the first listing you will find is a man named Hector Bravo and his free Wix website:

http://fontaneroguadalajara.wix.com/fontanero

Virtually by accident Mr. Bravo has been able to secure the top spot in one of the most competitive industries online and in one of the most advanced cities in Mexico. Hector Bravo is literally one of the luckiest plumbers in the world. He is sitting on a goldmine and he probably doesn't even know it.

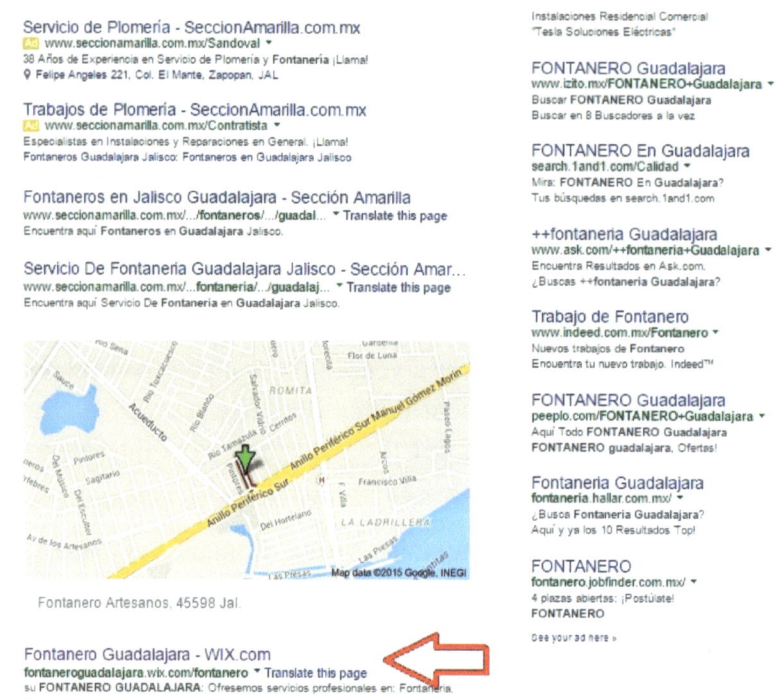

Just imagine what you can do with the right strategy, the right team of experts, and the proper implementation. With little work, you can easily rank on Google for multiple search terms and can generate leads and revenue easily and at a very low cost.

Online Advertising Costs

As Zack mentioned earlier in the proposal, one of the best parts of online advertising in the US in 2000 was the fact that the costs to drive traffic were so cheap. Well, as you'll see below the costs of advertising for a donut company in Mexico are extremely affordable and with fantastic results.

Within a 72 hour span, we ran a test for a fictitious Donut Company (named Donuts Guadalajara) in an attempt to generate leads. This company had no brand recognition whatsoever, no online reputation, and no product reviews. Furthermore, we did no testing of the ads or landing page and only targeted people in Guadalajara. It was the equivalent of online marketing in the US in the year 2000.

Our ads were run on Facebook to a landing page where the viewer could claim our coupon for "A Free Dozen Donuts" and you can see below the examples of each.

Facebook Ad:

Landing Page:

In that 72 hours, we were able to generate some pretty amazing results. In less than 3 days, our Free Dozen Donuts campaign generated 1216 Website Clicks, 923 Unique Visitors (some people clicked the ad more than once), and 369 Leads (ie. people who gave their email to receive the coupon).

Our conversion rate for this campaign 40% Conversion Rate which is typically only around 10% in the United States, our Cost per Click was only $.03 compared to around $.60 in the United States, and our Cost per Lead was only $.11 compared to around $50 in the United States. Our total spend for the campaign was only $39.91 to generate the 369 leads.

On top of the leads that were generated, the social engagement was also impressive. Our advertisement produced 192 Post Likes, 42 Shares, 33 Comments (Mostly people asking what's the address and when do you open), and 6 Facebook messages.

This proves that a) Facebook is a fantastic tool to generate leads for donuts and b) that people are yearning to connect and socialize with a donut company through Facebook.

WebsiteEn5Dias.com Solutions

As you can tell, the Mexican Online Marketplace provides many amazing opportunities for those willing to move quickly, however it also provides many challenges to those that do not have the proper understanding of the culture and digital landscape that make Mexico such a unique place.

Using our expertise in bringing American businesses into Mexico through Mexico Sales Made Easy and our web design, web management, and online marketing expertise via WebsiteEn5Dias.com, we would like to help your business expand its digital footprint into Mexico quickly and profitably.

Our proposal is to provide you the team of experts to help you implement the websites and marketing as well as the online support to provide each franchisee with a dedicated support team to help them grow their specific business in their local community.

Below is a list of the services that we provide.

1. **Establish a conversion-optimized and mobile-friendly website**

We create a Spanish custom websites for your business. Each site will be optimized to maximize leads and engagement and the Responsive Design will provide mobile users a great online experience.

2. **Optimize your local website for Google Search/SEO to dominate each local market before the competition increases**

We will provide Search Engine Optimization services for each local business so that they will achieve organic search ranking on Google.com.mx for their related search terms.

3. **Focus on building engagement on social media with photos and by starting conversations**

As we've proven in this proposal, Mexico is a social media driven country, which provides enormous opportunities for brands to connect with customers. Our team will help each location build their local social media reach by creating engagement through images and conversations online.

4. **Utilize Facebook advertising to drive high quality, low cost traffic to your website utilizing deals/specials**

As we've proven already, we can create significant lead generation with minimal investment for each local business. We will create similar advertising campaigns to help launch each new location, but also setup and manage other campaigns to continue lead-flow.

5. **Run Google Adwords on top YouTube channels**

Our team will also setup and manage Google Adwords on the top YouTube channels throughout Mexico. From creating the text ads, to setting up the targeting, to making adjustments to maximize engagement and ROI, each location will receive a dedicated team to help them capture leads and customers through YouTube

6. **Unlimited Online Marketing consulting to help you strategize on how to win**

As Mexican entrepreneurs begin to understand the power of social media and online marketing they will certainly have many questions as to why and how we are able to help them grow their franchise online. Our team of expert marketers and consultants will provide a hotline for your franchisees to call and get all of their questions and answered while also giving the ability to make changes to their website, social media, and marketing as needed.

7. **We provide the team of experts to build the online presence in Mexico.**

While, we the team of experts in Mexico, help your business succeed online in this new country and the personal attention and dedicated support team to the local franchises, the ultimate value that we provide to you is that we become your trusted partner to help your organization dominate the online landscape in Mexico quickly and with little effort. We provide a turnkey digital marketing solution to help manage all of your online needs in Mexico.

Conclusion

As with most things in business, having the proper team can mean the difference between success and failure. It's no different when building your web presence online in Mexico. While most of the online marketing tactics that we use in the U.S. will work incredibly well in Mexico, there are small nuances within the culture and online landscape that can make huge impacts on your ROI. If your team has the knowledge of the online culture of Mexico and you understand the language then by all means take this chapter and implement, implement, implement! There literally is no time to waste.

However, if your team lacks the skillset, manpower, and/or cultural expertise then let us launch your online presence in Mexico for you. There really is no second chance to make a first impression and wit the social reach in Mexico being so powerful your brand needs to put your best foot forward or the damage to your brand could take years to repair.

Whatever route you choose to take, Mexico is literally one of the best online opportunities in the entire world so I encourage your company to embrace this opportunity and make the most of this chance while it is still available.

CASE STUDIES

Mexico Franchising Made Easy has been fortunate to work with some amazingly fun and successful businesses. To capture the lessons and strategies along the way, I like to interview my clients or present them as case studies as a way to help others.

VIDBOX MEXICO

Interview with Daniel Ortega, Vice President of Sales for Vidbox Mexico

MSME: What does your company do?

DANIEL: We are based in Tijuana, Mexico and with the help of MFME, we have begun rolling out our business nationwide. We are a ground-breaking company that carries state-of-the-art automated retail kiosks that rents movies and video games. We are taking the success of Redbox and bringing it to Mexico.

MFME: Tell us in which way did MFME help you to accomplish your goals or objectives.

DANIEL: They have done everything for us to help launch the project the easiest, fastest way possible. They first assisted us with all the legal requirements to operate these types of machines in Mexico, they handled every single legal aspect of it. They even trademarked our name Vidbox and will handle all the equipment's importations and the logistics to place every kiosk on site. Not only that, they even placed us face to face with every single buyer from the largest chain stores in the country through their "CEO Tour" that they performed just a few months ago. Where else can you meet all of the buyers in a three-day period? It was fantastic.

MFME: Were you having any trouble before you started working with MFME?

DANIEL: They showed us the ABCs to doing business in Mexico and how to apply it to our specific market, worked together with us with the minimum details on commercial, marketing, legal and logistical fields.

They developed a system that allowed us to have the kiosks in Mexico for a price almost 35% under any other custom agency quotation, and half the time to import them – which provided us with huge savings. I would highly recommend using Mexperts for any enterprise wishing to do business in Mexico, particularly if you are clueless in Mexico business culture.

If you would like more information on Vidbox, please visit www.vidboxmexico.com.

Interview with Mathew Ilitch, Past President of Blue Line Foodservice Distribution

MATT: We handle the food distribution for Little Caesar's Pizza both in the USA and internationally and we are based in Farmington Hills, Michigan.

MFME: What trouble were you having with your business before contacting us?

MATT: There was no place to get complete information about how to ship to Mexico. We needed to know everything and we needed to do it without each franchise having to deal with different prices for supplies and the importing and distribution of those products.

MFME: What specifically did Mexperts do to help you?

MATT: They explained and executed the importing and distribution and helped us understand how to handle paper, supply and equipment deliveries the Little Caesar's stores throughout the country of Mexico. Now the handle the restaurant equipment logistics and now are opening a bonded warehouse which will save the franchises thousands of dollars in cash flow.

MFME: How else has Mexperts helped you do business in Mexico?

MATT: They keep us updated on new laws and regulations affecting our business in Mexico, well in advance of needing to make any changes. Their goals is to continuously improve our service to our franchisees, while lowering our costs.

If you would like more information on Blue Line Foodservice Distribution, please visit www.bluelinefd.com.

ALAN TAWIL WITH GLORIA JEAN'S COFFEES AND QUIZNOS SUBS

Alan Tawil is the master franchisor of Gloria Jean's Coffees and Quiznos Subs in Mexico. He sat down with us to share a few words on the process of bringing these world class franchises to Mexico.

Tell me a little about yourself:

I like to work and exercise, but I'm also a family man. I love spending time with my family and especially my nieces.

How did you get into franchising in Mexico?

My dad has always been dedicated to franchising, but he specialized in clothes and retail. I spent some time in Australia, and I loved going to Gloria Jean's Coffees. I loved it so much, I knew I wanted to bring it home with me, and that's how we decided to bring the brand to Mexico.

How did you hear about Mexico Franchising Made Easy?

I met Sandro through contacts of Nery's Logistics back when I was working with them. I've been working with Sandro for many years.

What has your experience with MFME been like?

My experience has been very pleasant. Sandro and MFME have been helping us with logistic consulting, marketing, franchise sales, and business strategy in Mexico.

What has MFME done to help you the most?

The MFME team knows a lot about marketing. That's where their knowledge has been the most useful. It's not just about exporting a franchise to Mexico, but selling it so people want to spend their money on your business.

What do you like most about doing business in Mexico?

I love doing business in Mexico, because it's an emerging country for economic expansion. It's a very large country, so there's a lot of room for growth.

Where do you see your business in the next 5-10 years?

In that time, I want to become one of the five biggest franchising companies in Mexico.

WHAT TO DO NOW

"How I look at Opportunities, I keep saying yes, until there is a reason to say NO! Sometimes it takes 15 seconds or 15 months of asking the right questions to say no."--Sandro Piancone

The methods and strategies that I've discussed throughout this book will help you to broaden and deepen your market. International expansion is just a border away, with one of the world's fastest growing affluent societies on our doorstep.

Everything I've written about within these pages has been tried and tested and honed to perfection, first through my own companies as they expanded their business and profits throughout Mexico, and then adding in the flexibility that individual clients need.

The answer to the original question posed at the start of this book - "Can I franchise my business in Mexico?" is a definite yes. Unfortunately I don't have the page space to recount all of the successes that Mexico Franchising Made Easy has achieved over the years. But if you'd like to know more, please feel free to drop me an email or contact the Mexperts at www.Mexicofranchisingmade easy.com

Of course, to ensure your company's success and its profits from your new Mexican customers you'll need to follow a plan and create a strategy for success.

Our office is in San Diego, California and should you wish to contact me directly about consulting, speaking, or just comment about the book please e-mail me at spiancone@mexicofranchisingmadeeasy.com or call my office at (619) 616-2973.

About the Author: Sandro Piancone

 Sandro is what might be called a serial entrepreneur. He started his first business at the age of ten, placing video games in retail outlets such as pizza shops, restaurants bars, and cafes for a friend of his fathers. The late 1970's were a great time for people in the video gaming business, and Sandro was paid $50 for each placement he made: big money back then, especially for one so young in business. Somehow, Sandro spotted the top of the market, took his profits, and moved to a more lucrative hobby and business: collecting comic books.

But that was back then. Having founded and built up several successful businesses since, he now describes himself as a 'recovering' CEO of a publicly trade foodservice company in Mexico. Sandro has introduced a number of US brands to Mexico, and helped to build them to multi-million dollar brands in the country: brand names such as Miller Beer, Thrifty Ice Cream, Roma Food, and Rockstar Energy Drinks. He sits on several corporate boards, advising on issues such as trademark and labeling requirements. Present clients include Little Caesars Pizza, Queso Nery's, Nery's Logistics, Vidbox and 5-hour Energy. Since 1998, he has generated well over 500 million dollars in sales and profits for his clients and partners helping them export their products into Mexico.

He works long and hard to make sure that his clients, and their products, move to market as quickly as possible with no hiccups.

You see, in his own businesses he's made all the mistakes that could possibly have been made when transitioning from the United States to Mexico. He's had product stopped at the Mexican border because the paperwork was fouled up. But only once. He's seen his product sales hit by unfair competition issues inside Mexico. But only once. Every time he's made a mistake, he's learned from it.

It's this experience, a dedication to great customer care, and an attitude of providing flawless execution of tasks that he not only brings to Mexico Franchising Made Easy, but also instills amongst all his staff.

While not travelling throughout Mexico, Sandro lives in San Diego with his amazing wife Kim, and his 2 cute M&Ms. He enjoys collecting rare "signed first edition" books (both comic books and auto-biographies.)

His office is in San Diego, California and should you wish to contact him directly about consulting, speaking, or just comment about the book please e-mail him at spiancone@mexicofranchisingmadeeasy.com or call his offices at (619) 616-2973.

How to Reach Your Free Gifts?

FREE - Newsletter $99 value
www.mexicosalesmadeeasy.com/freenewsletter.html

FREE Trademark Search in Mexico $249
www.mexicosalesmadeeasy.com/trademark.html

FREE - Special Report -
3 Things you absolutely need to do before selling in Mexico

FREE - Special Report -
Top 5 Reasons your product will get stuck at the border

www.mexicosalesmadeeasy.com/report.html